The ESSENTIAL WIZARD of OZ

DEDICATION

In 1880, Maud Gage enrolled at Cornell University as one among nineteen women in the freshman class. Sophomore-year roommate Josie Baum introduced Maud to her cousin, Lyman Frank Baum, an actor in a traveling theater troupe, and at twenty years of age, she sacrificed further education to accept Baum's marriage proposal. While he went on to write *The Wizard of Oz* and its sequels, Maud managed the family affairs and raised their four boys through the ups and downs of her husband's career. This book is as much dedicated to her memory as it is dedicated to all the women behind important men.

10/31/38
original Dress-
own Hair & fall
before darkening

OZ AND ENDS

An orphaned girl living on a farm in Kansas gets whisked off into a magical world at the other end of the rainbow.

This year marks a milestone in motion picture history – the 75th anniversary of Metro-Goldwyn-Mayer's *The Wizard of Oz*. And given its ubiquity in popular culture and its place in the hearts of generations of moviegoers, one wonders, after all this time, if there could be anything more we don't already know about it. But no matter how familiar the images, how memorable the music, how timeless the story, the answer is, yes, there's a whole book worth of things most of us will be surprised to learn. You're holding that book in your hands.

The Essential Wizard of Oz is brimming with amazing true stories, corrected myths, and particular particulars about the most-watched movie in film history – more than one billion people have seen it. It's not meant to provide a comprehensive nor complete academic reference, but rather an accessible distillation, a delightful confection in its own right, about a film that is one of the most beloved pieces of motion picture art and one that has resonated across three-quarters of a century.

Browse through this little book to satisfy your curiosity. It's guaranteed to reveal things you never knew about *The Wizard of Oz*.

— Horace Martin Woodhouse

In 1900, author Lyman Frank Baum of Chittenango, New York partnered with illustrator William Wallace Denslow to publish *The Wonderful Wizard of Oz*. It remained the best-selling children's book in America for two years after initial publication, was translated into some 40 languages, and spawned numerous sequels. In 1914, Baum formed the Oz Film Manufacturing Company and produced five silent-era features and a few short subjects based on the *Oz* books. On January 26, 1934, Baum's oldest son, Frank Joslyn Baum, sold off the family's rights to *The Wonderful Wizard of Oz* to independent film producer Samuel Goldwyn for a flat $40,000. There was no provision for royalties, even if the film did well.

Samuel Goldwyn had plans for developing an *Oz* film with eye-rolling, song-and-dance man Eddie Cantor as the Scarecrow and Ziegfeld Follies comedian Ed Wynn as the Wizard. However, Cantor was committed to *Roman Scandals* and Wynn showed little interest in "a mere cameo role," so the project was shelved. In 1937, 20th Century Fox studio attempted to secure Goldwyn's film rights as a vehicle for reigning child star Shirley Temple, but was outbid by the MGM studio which, on February 18, 1938, plunked down a hefty $75,000 for exclusive rights. (The hated Goldwyn was ousted from his own company before the merger orchestrated by Marcus Loew — why his name became part of Metro-Goldwyn-Mayer, even though he himself had nothing to do with the company).

Released in 1937, *Snow White and the Seven Dwarfs* grossed $3.5 million in the U.S. and an additional $6.5 million internationally. In the wake of its boffo box office, MGM set out to "borrow" from the *Snow White* formula (innocent young heroine, powerful villainess, comical sidekicks), and similarities are all too obvious. The song "We're Off to See the Wizard" was written in the spirit of Disney's "Heigh Ho." A minor character in Baum's book, the role of the Wicked Witch of the West was expanded for the film, similar to the Queen in *Snow White*. It should be noted that Baum did not describe only the Munchkins as short in stature, but rather it was the norm for all of the inhabitants of Oz — the film's Munchkins were a response to Disney's "Seven Dwarfs."

B efore the property landed at MGM, Walt Disney had his own eye on Baum's story as an animated feature, and his research team floated the idea of Mickey Mouse in the Dorothy role, transported to Oz along with Donald Duck, Pluto, and Goofy.

B orn into a musical family (her father taught music in New York City and her mother sang at the Royal Opera), Adriana Mitchell Caselotti was 18 years old and working as a chorus girl when Walt Disney personally chose her for the voice of Snow White in *Snow White and the Seven Dwarfs*, for which she was paid a total of $970. Uncredited for her work in *Oz*, Caselotti was the voice of "Juliet" during the Tin Man's song, "If I Only Had a Heart," with the line, "Wherefore art thou, Romeo." (That's also her singing voice in Frank Capra's 1946 classic, *It's a Wonderful Life*, during George Bailey's anguished prayer in Martini's Bar).

Louis B. Mayer, the feisty, cigar-chomping czar who ruled his kingdom with an iron fist, built MGM into the most financially successful motion picture studio in the world and, by the way, the only one to pay dividends throughout the Great Depression. Mayer envisioned W.C. Fields as the Wizard, but ran out of patience after protracted haggling over his demand for $100,000 to play the role. (Fields once said, "A rich man is nothing but a poor man with money). Frank Morgan, who earned $1,500 a week as a contract player, was cast instead. According to a letter from Fields' agent, the timing wasn't right – the "Great Man" was too busy writing the screenplay for *You Can't Cheat an Honest Man* (scripted by Fields under the pseudonym "Charles Bogle").

Frank Morgan was born Francis Phillip Wuppermann, the youngest in a family that earned its wealth distributing Angostura Bitters, permitting Frank to attend Cornell. He dropped out of the university in 1909 after only a year of study to follow his older brother Ralph into show business, first on the Broadway stage and then into motion pictures. MGM producers didn't consider Morgan for the part until he begged for a screen test. Different make-ups were tested for his role as the Wizard, and a final look was reached after at least five tries. In the film, the 49-year-old Morgan also portrays Professor Marvel, the Gatekeeper, the Mayor/Carriage Driver, the Guard, and the disembodied Wizard head.

For the role of Dorothy, there was initial interest in Charlotte Henry who had earlier appeared *Alice in Wonderland* with W. C. Fields and *Babes in Toyland* with Laurel and Hardy. Producers Mervyn LeRoy and Arthur Freed wanted sixteen-year-old Judy Garland to play the central character, but Nicholas Schenck, the president of MGM's parent company, Loew's, concerned with the financial scale of the *Oz* project, questioned whether Judy could carry the film (and she was almost too old to play Dorothy). He preferred eleven-year-old Shirley Temple, the biggest box office draw in Hollywood at the time, and encouraged Louis B. Mayer to borrow her from Darryl F. Zanuck at 20th Century Fox to play Dorothy. Zanuck, however, refused to release her from her contract obligations to have her work for "the enemy." Bonita Granville and Deanna Durbin were briefly considered, but Garland was cast.

Producer Mervyn LeRoy was a short, gregarious man who grew up on vaudeville from the age of 14 and believed that "the aim of movies is to entertain." He read widely to find fresh material, and said that a successful film "had to be believable and have a good, solid story and the quality I call 'heart.'" Arthur Freed began his career as a song-plugger and pianist in Chicago and also wrote material for the Marx Brothers. He was eventually hired by MGM, and after serving as the associate producer for *Oz*, he went on to produce many of the greatest musicals in Hollywood history. As producers, the two men complimented each other – LeRoy focused on direction, camera work, and special effects, while Freed handled the music, art direction, set design, and costuming. (It was LeRoy's daring idea to shoot the scenes when Dorothy in black-and-white and the Land of Oz scenes in color).

After his refusal to loan Shirley Temple to MGM, Darryl F. Zanuck hastily assembled his own fairy-tale vehicle for the young star. *The Blue Bird*, adapted from the allegorical stage play by Maurice Maeterlinck, was shot in Technicolor for the fantasy "body" of the film and bookended with black-and-white sequences, a blatant imitation of *Oz*. Gale Sondergaard, the first choice to play the Wicked Witch of the West in *Oz*, was cast as *Blue Bird*'s villainess. Despite its flop at the box office, the film received Oscar nominations for Best Cinematography and Best Special Effects.

When MGM bought the rights to Baum's book, it also purchased the rights to Larry Semon's 1925 silent version of *Oz* for Chadwick Pictures, featuring Semon's wife Dorothy Dwan as Dorothy Gale and a young Oliver Hardy (pre-Laurel and Hardy) as the Tin Man. That film took a number of liberties with the original plot. It introduced Miss Gulch, the three farmhands (Hunk, Hickory and Zeke) and the bogus but kind-hearted fortuneteller, Professor Marvel, characters who do not appear in any of Baum's books.

In the Baum books, there is no hint that Oz is anything but a real place, to which Dorothy returns in later adventures, but the filmmakers felt the need to make the story acceptable to adults. Dorothy's journey was explained at the end as a dream, and the film constantly emphasizes the unreality of Oz — with talking trees, little people, and flying monkeys.

During pre-production, there was some debate about whether the Wicked Witch of the West should be portrayed as an ugly witch or a glamorous villainess (like the Wicked Queen in *Snow White*). Gale Sondergaard was originally cast for the part and tested with the two different looks. After the decision was made in favor of "ugly" (Glinda says "Only bad witches are ugly"), Sondergaard, reluctant to wear the disfiguring makeup, withdrew from the role. After considering Edna May Oliver (who it is said always looked as though she had flown in on a broomstick), the part went to 37-year-old character actress Margaret Hamilton. A life-long fan of the *Oz* books, Hamilton was ecstatic when she learned the producers were interested in her. When she phoned her agent to find out what role she was up for, her agent replied, "The witch, who else?"

Louis B. Mayer's constant derision of Judy's appearance made her feel extremely insecure. She was told she was too short, too chubby, and had no neck. He called her his "little hunchback," and insisted that while the screenplay was being prepared she was to go on alternate days of fasting. He sent orders to the studio commissary explaining that Judy was to be fed nothing but chicken soup. However, she would often smuggle in double portions of mashed potatoes and gravy from the commissary kitchen. In desperation, studio handlers resorted to their last option – diet pills.

Benzedrine or "bennies" not only suppressed appetite, they increased energy and helped a performer's endurance. In a 1963 article for *McCall's Magazine*, Judy explained, "When we were in production, they had us working days and nights on end. They'd give us pep pills to keep us on our feet long after we were exhausted. Then they'd take us to the studio hospital and knock us cold with sleeping pills. Then, after four hours, they'd wake us up and give us the pep pills again so we could work another 72 hours in a row." Thus began a vicious cycle that would persist her entire life.

A number of adjustments were necessary to transform Judy into Dorothy, most of them intended to make her look younger. As the lead character in *Oz*, she was supposed to be a young girl, however Judy was developing into a woman, and it showed. In order to make her fit the character, she was bound and corseted to flatten her bosom, and her blue gingham dress was fitted for its blurring effect on her figure. (Judy barely topped five feet, and with tall co-stars, she looked even smaller).

Throughout the 1930s, Harold Arlen teamed with lyricist Ted Koehler to write shows for New York's Cotton Club, as well as Broadway musicals and Hollywood films. Their partnership resulted in familiar standards including "Let's Fall in Love" and "Stormy Weather." Edgar Yipsel "Yip" Harburg wrote the lyrics to "April in Paris," "It's Only a Paper Moon," and "Brother, Can You Spare a Dime?" (a song that became an anthem of the Great Depression). MGM gave Arlen and Harburg fourteen weeks and the keys to a studio bungalow to come up with songs to develop the characters and advance the plot of *Oz*, a practice that was unusual for films at that time. They were paid $25,000, with one-third advanced against royalties. ("We're Off to See the Wizard" took on a special meaning during World War II. During the invasion of Normandy, Allied troops sang a parody called "We're Off to See Herr Hitler").

Composers Arlen and Harburg had already discussed the theme of a rainbow as the bridge from one place to another — from the Kansas farm to the Land of Oz — when Arlen was on his way to see a movie at Grauman's Chinese Theater in Hollywood. He was passing Schwab's Pharmacy on Sunset Boulevard, a popular hangout for movie actors and movie industry dealmakers, when he asked his wife to stop the car so he could jot down a tune. The melody of "Over the Rainbow" was composed in Arlen's car parked outside the front door of Schwab's.

"That song has to go," insisted MGM executives. "Over the Rainbow" was initially deleted from the film after a preview in San Luis Obispo, because Louis B. Mayer and producer Mervyn LeRoy thought the song "slowed down the picture" and that "it sounds like something for Jeanette MacDonald, not for a little girl singing in a barnyard." The persistence of associate producer Arthur Freed and Judy's vocal coach/mentor Roger Edens restored the song in the film. (Rarely have song and singer been so ideally matched, and according to Harold Arlen, "Judy had the ability to project a song and a voice that penetrated your insides. She sang not just to your ears, but to your tear ducts.")

In 1939, after serving as associate producer of *Oz*, Arthur Freed was promoted to the head of his own unit within MGM, helping to elevate the studio to the leading creator of film musicals. His first solo credit as producer was the film version of Rodgers and Hart's Broadway musical *Babes in Arms*. It starred Mickey Rooney and Judy Garland, and it was so successful that it ushered in a long series of "let's put on a show" musicals starring Rooney and Garland. (Filming of *Babes in Arms* began on May 12, 1939, soon after Judy had finished filming *Oz*, and was completed on July 18, 1939. The film premiered on October 13, 1939).

Before signing her for *Oz*, David O. Selznick considered Judy Garland for the role of Carreen, the youngest of Scarlett O'Hara's three sisters, in *Gone With the Wind*. The part instead went to Ann Rutherford, who appears early in the film, begging to go to the ball at Ashley Wilkes' plantation. "Oh, Mother, can't I stay up for the ball tomorrow? ... I'm 13 now." At first, Louis B. Mayer refused her the role, calling it "a nothing part," but Rutherford, who was a fan of the novel, burst into tears in his office and Mayer relented. Rutherford later played Andy Hardy's girlfriend Polly Benedict in the comedy series with Mickey Rooney.

There are many clear instances in which the plot in the film differs from the original Baum book. Most notable was that in the books, Oz was a real place, while it was only a dream in the film. In a later book, Auntie Em and Uncle Henry take refuge in Oz when they can't pay the mortgage on the new house built after the tornado removed their first house (which is miraculously intact at the end of the film). MGM also toned down some of Baum's gore, notably in passages describing "Kalidahs" (tiger-bear hybrids) being dashed to pieces, the Tin Woodman decapitating wolves with his axe, and bumblebees stinging themselves to death.

Adrian Adolph Greenberg, who called himself Adrian, was MGM's chief costume designer. He had read Baum's *Oz* books in his youth, and as he pondered costumes for the film, he had his sister send him his boyhood sketchbooks, filled with whimsical drawings of the inhabitants of Oz. He would eventually create 3,210 individual sketches for the costumes. (Adrian is credited with creating the padded shoulder fashion trend that became the "trademark" of Joan Crawford). Although he was openly gay, Adrian married actress Janet Gaynor (the first winner of the Academy Award for Best Actress) in 1939.

Multiple styles of shoes were tested by the MGM wardrobe department before they settled on the low schoolgirl-style pumps with bows. The iconic ruby slippers were made by Joe Napoli at the Western Costume Company. (By the time Adrian came to design them, the color had changed from the book's silver slippers to red at the suggestion of screenwriter Noel Langley in order to show up more vividly against the Yellow Brick Road). As was customary for important props, a number of pairs were made for the film, although no one knows exactly how many. Judy requested one pair a half-size larger, so she would be more comfortable in the afternoon when her feet were slightly swollen from the rigors of the morning rehearsals and filming.

To create the ruby slippers, white satin pumps were dyed burgundy and covered with tonally-matched sequined organza. Adrian added butterfly-shaped red strap leather, Art Deco-inspired bows, each with three large, rectangular, red-glass jewels and dark red bugle beads, outlined in red glass rhinestones in silver settings. The stones and beads were sewn to the bows, then to the shoe. Orange felt was glued to the soles to deaden the sound of Judy dancing on the Yellow Brick Road. (In one sequence, Judy is not wearing the ruby slippers — an apparent blunder by the filmmakers. As the apple trees pelt the Scarecrow with apples, she is briefly seen wearing black shoes).

For Dorothy's dress and blouse, Adrian experimented with many different versions and variations, including a red dress as well as an all-blue dress. An early version of the blouse included blue bows on the sleeves and collar. The design team created several prototypes for Dorothy's dress, but in the end simply went back to Baum's description in the book: "It was gingham, with checks of white and blue." (While the checkered jumper worn in the film is often thought to be blue and white, it's actually blue and light pink).

MGM's first roaring lion mascot, Jackie, appeared on all black-and-white MGM films from 1928 to 1956, as well as the sepia-tinted opening credits of *Oz*. Jackie growled softly, followed by a louder roar, a brief pause, and then a final growl, before he looked off to the right of the screen. (He was housed on the MGM studio lot in digs that amounted to an onsite zoo). Producer Mervyn LeRoy had originally intended to use Leo in the role of the Cowardly Lion and dub an actor's voice in for the dialogue. However, that idea was dropped when Bert Lahr became available for the part.

While singing "If I Were King," the Lion asks, "What makes the Sphinx the Seventh Wonder?" The Sphinx is actually not one of the Seven Wonders of the World; that distinction belongs to its neighbor, the Great Pyramid of Giza. The line "What makes the dawn come up like thunder?" in the Lion's speech about courage is a reference to a line in the Rudyard Kipling poem *Mandalay*: "An' the dawn comes up like thunder outer China 'crost the Bay!"

The original cross-shaped Courage Medal prop was made of poly-chromed metal, featuring a lion in profile above a crown, a knight's helmet, and the word "Courage" in raised blue scroll lettering. In the late 1950s, Mal Caplan, head of the costume department at MGM, was in a life-threatening automobile accident, and spent months in the hospital before returning to work. His colleagues and the management at MGM presented him with the original Cowardly Lion's Courage Medal. (He was also given the Tin Man's "heart," but he gave it away to a man in the same hospital who was having open heart surgery).

Clara Blandick, who played Auntie Em, filmed all her scenes in one week. (Auntie Em and Uncle Henry are the only characters from the beginning of the movie not to have alter ego characters in the Land of Oz). Blandick beat out character actresses May Robson, Janet Beecher, and Sarah Padden for the role, and earned $750 for her work. Although her character proved memorable to audiences, few know Blandick's name. She is not billed in the opening credits and is listed last in the movie's closing credits.

Born in Xenia, Ohio, young Charley Ellsworth Grapewin ran away from home to join the circus. He worked as an aerialist and trapeze artist with the famous P. T. Barnum circus troupe before turning to acting. Beginning in the silent era, he appeared in more than one hundred films, including *The Good Earth*, *The Grapes of Wrath*, and *Tobacco Road*. Grapewin came out of retirement to play Uncle Henry in *Oz*. (Uncle Henry is the only character whose role is limited to the Kansas sequence).

Similar in height and build to Judy, but with bigger feet, twenty-year-old Caren Marsh was her dance stand-in. A special pair of ruby slippers was made for her. She would also serve as a stand-in for Judy a second time with *Ziegfeld Girl* in 1941. (In 1957, Marsh married Bill Doll, a press agent to producer Mike Todd).

All the film's sequences were filmed in three-strip Technicolor, except the Kansas scenes which were shot on black-and-white film, then soaked in a sepia toning bath. When Dorothy opens the door, it is not Judy but her stunt-double, Bobbie Koshay, wearing a sepia gingham dress, who backs out of the frame. Once the camera moves through the door, Judy steps out of her monochrome Midwest into the frame wearing her blue gingham dress and emerges from the house's shadow into the full Technicolor of Munchkinland. At the moment when brown-and-white turns to color, a few frames on the film required hand painting to give the transition a smooth effect. (Sepia was also used in the scene where Aunt Em appears in the Wicked Witch's crystal ball).

The film had six different directors. With a reputation for working with younger performers (including Jackie Cooper and Deanna Durbin), director Norman Taurog worked on early test footage and was paid for three days of directorial work. He was replaced by Richard Thorpe who directed the next two weeks of filming, including Judy Garland as Dorothy in a blonde wig with "baby-doll" makeup that made her look like anything but an innocent Kansas farm girl. Thorpe was re-assigned to *The Adventures of Huckleberry Finn*, and director George Cukor was brought in as "creative advisor." He jettisoned the wig and heavy makeup before the production was re-started with Victor Fleming at the helm. Instead of completing the film, Fleming replaced Cukor in *Gone With the Wind*'s own game of musical director's chairs, and King Vidor shot the remainder of the film, mainly the Kansas sequences. Reportedly, Mervyn LeRoy also directed some transitional scenes, joining the round-robin of directors who worked on the movie.

Judy had a habit of bursting into laughter during takes. When this occurred during the scene where Dorothy slaps the Cowardly Lion, Victor Fleming, a serious and intimidating director, came up to Judy and slapped her across the face and sent her to her dressing room. Upon her return, Judy did the scene in one take and without laughing. In the film, she can still be seen to be stifling a smile between the lines "Well, of course not" and "My, what a fuss you're making."

Screenwriter Herman L. Manckiewicz, who later co-wrote *Citizen Kane* with Orson Welles, turned in the first draft of the *Oz* screenplay. At least three other screenwriting "teams" were also hired, each without knowledge of the others, and the final mish-mash of a script was worked on by more than a dozen writers, including Noel Langley, Florence Ryerson, Edgar Allan Woolf, Irving Brecher, William H. Cannon, Herbert Fields, Arthur Freed, E.Y. Harburg, Samuel Hoffenstein, John Lee Mahin, Jack Mintz, Ogden Nash, Sid Silvers, as well as Jack Haley and Bert Lahr for additional dialogue. (Louis B. Mayer once said, "The number one book of the ages was written by a committee, and it was called The Bible").

Noel Langley was chosen as screenwriter on the basis of his book, *The Tale of the Land of Green Ginger*, a children's novel concerning the son of Aladdin, first published in 1937. Although most of his ideas were used in the finished film, and he is credited as being the principal screenwriter, there were a number of unauthorized revisions to his material. Langley was incensed that they had been done, and walked out on the project several times, although he was always persuaded to return. He was bitterly resentful of the final screenplay, and is on record as saying that he hated the finished film when he finally saw it.

In early drafts of the script, the writers came up with a few ideas that were (thankfully) scrapped. There might have been an opera-singing Princess Betty of Oz, a son of the Wicked Witch with ambitions to be King of Oz, a niece for Miss Gulch, a rescue from the Wizard's balloon by the Munchkin fire department, and a "Rainbow Bridge" that the Witch constructs as a trap for Dorothy. In one suggested version, there were hints that Dorothy would develop a relationship with Hunk, the real-world counterpart to the Scarecrow, with him leaving for agricultural college at the end of the movie, but getting Dorothy's promise to write to him. (The relationship wasn't completely eliminated from the final screenplay, however, most notably when Dorothy says to the Scarecrow, "I think I'll miss you most of all.")

The legendary "Jitterbug" was a musical number that was part of an abandoned subplot in the film. It was intended to add appeal to a younger audience who had embraced the era's swing dance craze. As the song begins, Dorothy and her three companions see a jitterbug flitting in the shadows from tree to tree and become frightened (there is actually no such insect as a jitterbug). The refrain they sing is: "Oh, the bats and the bees and the breeze in the trees have a terrible, horrible buzz. So, be careful of that rascal — keep away from the Jitterbug." The Jitterbug puts a magical influence on the characters, forcing them to dance. Soon there are many jitterbugs, and eventually, everyone collapses from exhaustion. (A reference to the Jitterbug sequence survives in the Wicked Witch's orders to Nikko the leader of the Flying Monkeys, when she tells him to "send the insects on ahead to take the fight out of them."

It was the task of producer Mervyn LeRoy to whittle down the film's excessive running time of 120 minutes. After a preview in San Bernadino, LeRoy cut the "Jitterbug" number and the Scarecrow's extended dance sequence (choreographed by legendary innovator Busby Berkeley). A second preview in Pomona, where the film ran 112 minutes, LeRoy cut a reprise of "Over The Rainbow" and a scene in which the Tin Man turns into a human beehive. By the third preview in San Luis Obispo, the film was down to its 101-minute running time, where it has remained ever since.

All early Technicolor films were overseen by a consultant from the company. When Harold G. "Hal" Rosson, a cinematographer known for his imaginative lighting, was assigned to *Oz*, he had the assistance of two consultants lent to MGM by Technicolor, including Henri Jaffa, who clashed with designer Adrian over the colors of the Munchkin costumes. (Rosson met Jean Harlow when he shot her wig tests for *Red-Headed Woman*. They eloped to Yuma, Arizona on September 13, 1933 during location shooting for *Bombshell*. The marriage lasted seven months — Harlow accused him of "mental cruelty" for reading in bed).

The Technicolor Corporation began making color movies as early as 1917, but the high cost and complexity of the method kept color films from becoming the standard for several decades. *Oz* was only the second film MGM had made in three-strip Technicolor, then a new technology. Technicolor required lights of blazing intensity since film passed through the cameras so slowly, so much power, in fact, that Southern California Edison had to install a small substation on the MGM property.

In 1929, Herbert Stothart was signed to a contract by Louis B. Mayer. The composer spent the next twenty years at MGM, composing, arranging, adapting, and conducting scores for over 100 features, including *Oz*. Stothart composed the background music for the film, as well as leading the studio orchestra in synchronizing the music with the on-screen action. Title music shows influences from both Ravel and Debussy. His score includes several classical music references, including snippets of Mussorgsky's "Night on Bald Mountain," Schumann's "The Happy Farmer" and a Mendelssohn piano sonata (when Toto escapes from the Wicked Witch of the West).

Working under Stothart's guidance, George Bassman (who composed music for the Marx Brothers' films *A Day at the Races*, *Go West*, and *The Big Store*) orchestrated the background music and also composed some pieces of music for the film. Most notably, Bassman composed the one and a half minutes of music that accompany the tornado sequence, a task that took him three weeks. As a joke, Bassman stuck in six bars of the 1905 tune, "In the Shade of the Old Apple Tree," when the talking apple trees become angry with Dorothy for picking their fruit. (In 1947, Bassman admitted that he had been a member of the Communist party and found himself blacklisted by the film industry).

The film's violin solo was performed by Russian virtuoso violinist Toscha Seidel, known for the lush, romantic tones he added to motion picture productions throughout the 1930s. In 1934 Seidel gave violin instruction to Albert Einstein, and received a sketch in return, reportedly diagramming length contraction of his theory of relativity.

Jack Martin Smith was the assistant art director and production designer. He served as the film's primary sketch artist, transferring the concepts of his bosses, Cedric Gibbons and Bill Horning, into artwork for further realization by the studio's construction department. Smith produced all blueprint plans used on the film, plus color sketches (measuring two by three feet) of all the sixty-plus sets. Gibbons, head of the art department, rejected Smith's colors as too bright, and demanded a more subdued, "ethereal" pallet. Smith did all the sketch-work over a second time.

Head of the MGM art department, Cedric Gibbons oversaw the work of art director Bill Horning, although Gibbons is personally credited with the design concept of Emerald City. Gibbons' team conceived and built the two main areas for Munchkinland and Oz. Sixty-five different sets covered six soundstages and 25 acres of the studio backlot. Munchkinland alone consisted of 122 structures, one-fourth normal size. Gibbons approved and signed (or rejected) every drawing done on every MGM film, including all of the drawings for *Oz* by Jack Martin Smith. (Gibbons was a founding member of the Academy of Motion Picture Arts and Sciences, and he supervised the design of the Oscar statuette.)

Warren A. Newcombe's specialty at MGM was matte painting, a technique that provided backgrounds to scenes and shots that could not be economically accomplished with any other technique – most notably Emerald City. (Although L. Frank Baum made his home in Chicago, he preferred to winter in Coronado, California, across the bay from San Diego, where he did much of his writing at the Hotel del Coronado, a turn-of-the-century seaside resort. It has been speculated that the hotel's whimsical design with fanciful red roofs and spires was his inspiration for Emerald City).

Most actors on the five-month shoot (from October 1938 to March 1939) worked six days a week and had to arrive at the studio at four and five in the morning to be fitted with makeup and costumes and worked until seven or eight at night. To assist with the makeup demands, MGM recruited extra help from the studio mail room and courier service. As most of the extras required prosthetic devices (false ears, noses, etc.), and since application of prosthetics requires extensive training, each recruit was instructed in one area of prosthetic application from station to station along an assembly line. Any discomfort of makeup or costume was compounded by the heat from the extensive lighting on the set (required by the early Technicolor process), often at over a hundred degrees.

Austrian entrepreneur Baron Leopold von Singer assembled a troupe of "midgets" (the term is now widely considered pejorative) who performed in vaudeville shows throughout Europe and America. MGM contracted with Singer to provide 124 of his "little people" to play the Munchkins (Baum never explained where the term came from). Singer charged each actor a 50 percent commission on their $100 per week salary. During filming, the MGM commissary was overrun with bottom-pinching Munchkins. The studio arranged to house Singer's troupe in the Culver Hotel, located near the studio lot. Chambermaids at the hotel were said to be in fear of their lives. Mervyn Leroy explained, "They got into fights and sex orgies at the hotel. Nearly every night the Culver City police were called to the hotel." (As a result of the popularity of *Oz*, the word "munchkin" has entered the English language as a reference to small children).

The Munchkins didn't do their own singing. Their numbers were recorded by the children's choir from St. Joseph's Church in Los Angeles, then played back at a faster speed, with the orchestra added to those takes. Ken Darby, whose choral group sang backup for Bing Crosby on the original 1942 recording of "White Christmas," provided vocals for the Munchkinland Mayor. Munchkin speaking parts were dubbed in by voice actors, including "Pinto" Colvig (Disney's bark for Pluto and voice of Goofy), Billy Bletcher (the voice of Tom the cat of *Tom and Jerry*), and Abe Dinovitch (who also provided the voice of the talking apple tree).

With a background as a salesman and fairground barker, Meinhardt Frank Raabe was cast as one of the more prominent Munchkins. His character, the Coroner, announces that the Wicked Witch of the East is "not only merely dead, she's really most sincerely dead." The date listed on her death certificate is actually the date of L. Frank Baum's death, May 6, 1919. (Raabe was, at one time, the shortest licensed pilot in the U.S. During WWII, he volunteered for military service, and after being turned down, he worked as an instructor in the Civil Air Patrol).

Jerry Maren was born Gerard Marenghi in Boston, Massachusetts. A three-foot-four-inch dwarf, he played the member of the Lollipop Guild who clasps his hands over his head triumphantly after handing over the lollipop to Dorothy. In the scene where Glinda floats away in the bubble, Maren chases after it. In the 1950s, Maren portrayed "Little Oscar" for the Oscar Mayer Company, "Buster Brown" in television and radio commercials, and Mayor McCheese in commercials for McDonald's. (*Seinfeld* aficionados may recall Maren as the aging circus performer father of Kramer's buddy Mickey in "The Yada Yada" episode).

A dwarf who stood three-feet-eight-inches tall, Pat Walshe was a vaudeville animal impersonator. As well as being able to act like animals, he also could imitate their sounds. Due to his specialized skill and short stature, he was given the part of Nikko, leader of the Winged Monkeys. (The monkeys are apparently intelligent enough to obey commands, but do not speak, making them seem less benign). "Nikko" is listed in the credits, even though his character was never referred to by name in the film. (The original 17th century carving of the three wise monkeys, "see no evil, hear no evil, speak no evil," is located in Nikko, Japan).

Mitchell Lewis appeared in 200 films between 1914 and 1956. His best known role as Captain of the Winkie Guards was uncredited in *Oz*. His lines were "She's dead. You killed her. Hail to Dorothy! The Wicked Witch is dead!" and, in response to Dorothy's request for the late witch's broomstick, "Please! And take it with you!" The other Winkie Guard actors were Robert St. Angelo (who played a Roman soldier in the original *King of Kings*), Phil Harron (cast as one of the "Lionians" in *Tarzan and the Slave Girl*), and Harry Wilson (whose distinctive facial features were the result of a disorder of the pituitary gland).

The three pink-clad ballerinas of the Lullabye League were Nita Krebs (who made her living as a dancer until her retirement in the mid-1950s), Olga Nardone (known as "Little Olga" and "Princess Olga" was one of the smallest of the Munchkins, standing at just 3 foot 4 inches), and Yvonne Bistany Moray (who was called "a smaller version of Greta Garbo" by her friends in the cast).

Although just twenty-four inches tall, Jeane La Barbera performed as a concert violist (with a custom-fitted instrument) in venues that included the London Palladium and the Hippodrome in New York. In *Oz*, Little Jeane was one of the tiniest Munchkin maidens. Because she was so small, director Victor Fleming inserted her in all the Munchkinland scenes, regardless of shot continuity. (After the close of shooting for the film, she was one of several Munchkins MGM retained for the publicity tour).

Munchkin sketches were part of Adrian's 3,210 individual drawings for costumes in the film. Under his direction, the studio wardrobe department designed over one hundred flower-adorned felt ensembles for the Munchkin sequences. His crew then had to photograph and catalog each Munchkin in his or her costume so that they could correctly apply the same costume and makeup each day of production.

At the end of the sequence in which Dorothy and the Scarecrow first meet the Tin Man, there is a disturbance in the trees. In perhaps the most bizarre urban legend in *Oz* folklore, this is believed to be one of the crew (or by some accounts, one of the dwarf actors) hanging himself, but it is actually one of the live exotic birds placed throughout the set. The bird lifts his head up, puts his head down, brings it back up, then spreads its wings, giving the illusion of someone swinging. A small toucan is visible in the tree (where the Witch is hiding) at the opening of this scene, and at least one Sarus Crane appears behind the Tin Man. (During the filming, one of the cranes attacked Ray Bolger's straw stuffing – so much for the Scarecrow's effectiveness at scaring birds).

Although many of the costumes were uncomfortable for the actors, Bert Lahr's was the most smothering. His heavily-padded Lion costume, made from the pelts of real lions, weighed over 50 pounds, and with temperatures on the set often reaching over 100 degrees, Lahr would sweat so profusely that the costume would be soaked by the end of the day. After takes, he would take it off, and both he and the costume were blasted with air from blow dryers to cool him down and make the costume wearable for the next shot. The Lion's mane consisted of a full-length wig with rubber ears sewn into the top, augmented with a separate beard under the actor's chin. A second version of the wig was needed after the Lion receives his permanent wave in the Emerald City beauty salon. His tail was suspended by a fishing line and worked by a crewmember from a catwalk above.

While performing as Jack Haley's Tin Man stunt-double, an overly exuberant Ambrose "Amblin' Amby" Schindler pulled loose the Cowardly Lion's tail as they climbed toward a mountaintop castle to rescue Dorothy from The Wicked Witch of the West. The scene had to be re-shot. (A star quarterback for the USC Trojans, Schindler led the 1937 team in rushing, scoring and total offense).

A crystal ball is used by the Wicked Witch of the West to keep track of Dorothy and her companions as they travel down the Yellow Brick Road to Oz. In one scene, Auntie Em appears in the glass ball while Dorothy is being held captive in the witch's castle, only to fade out and be replaced by a frightening image of the Witch. The hand-blown glass ball, approximately 25 inches in diameter, was previously used as a prop in *The Mask of Fu Manchu* starring Boris Karloff and in *Chandu the Magician* with Bela Lugosi, both released in 1932. (The ball was purchased by Jay Walker, founder of priceline.com, and housed in the Walker Library of the History of Human Imagination).

The Prince Albert-style frock coat worn by Frank Morgan as Professor Marvel was selected from among several tattered coats the wardrobe crew had obtained off the rack of a secondhand shop in Los Angeles. It had a velvet collar with the nap (raised fuzzy surface) worn off, but provided the actor a perfect fit. While wearing the coat during rehearsals, Morgan discovered an inside label that read "Property of L. Frank Baum." That coat, it seems, had originally been made for Baum by a tailor in Chicago — the tailor verified it, and Baum's widow, Maud Gage Baum, did as well. She was given the coat after the movie wrapped.

She was the widow of Florenz Ziegfeld, "glorifier of the American girl" as impresario of the Ziegfeld Follies. In 1938, after receiving an Oscar nomination for her performance as Emily Kilbourne in *Merrily We Live*, 54-year-old Billie Burke was chosen to play Glinda, the Good Witch of the North. For her gown, MGM designer Adrian re-cycled the gown first worn by Jeanette MacDonald in *San Francisco*. There were some alterations, including sheer sleeves, on Glinda's costume, as well as more glitter around the bodice and the addition of large "butterflies." The trim around the bodice had some of the decorations removed from the original, and the sleeves were puffed up for Glinda. (Beatrice Lillie, Fanny Brice, Cora Witherspoon, and Gracie Fields were others considered for the role of Glinda).

"**I**'ll get you, my pretty, and your little dog, too!" That little dog, of course, was Toto, who consistently moves the plot forward by creating mischief. She was played by Carl Spitz's female Cairn Terrier, Terry, whose first major film appearance was as "Rags" in 1934's *Bright Eyes* with Shirley Temple. Terry's salary for *Oz* ($125 per week) was more than that of many human actors in the film (and also more than many working Americans at the time). She attended the film's premiere at Grauman's Chinese Theater and because of the popularity of the film, her real-life name was changed to Toto.

Carl Spitz was a German immigrant and student of Konrad Most, widely considered to be "The Father of Dog Training in America." Spitz opened the Hollywood Dog Training School in California in 1927, and he developed the method of using silent hand signals to direct his animals (although it was reported that it took 12 takes to have Terry run alongside the actors as they skipped down the Yellow Brick Road). She was injured when one of the Winkie guards accidentally stepped on her, breaking her foot. Terry spent two weeks recuperating at Judy Garland's residence, and the actress developed a close attachment to her. Judy wanted to adopt Terry, but Spitz wouldn't give her up, and the dog went on to appear in several more films. When she died on September 1, 1945, Spitz buried her behind his kennel in Studio City, however, expansion of the Ventura Freeway in 1958 destroyed her resting place.

Jack Nathan Weatherwax, member of the famous Weatherwax family of animal trainers, assisted Spitz with the training of Terry. He began his career as an animal trainer working for the Rennie Renfro Motion Picture Dogs before taking up with his brothers in the 1940s as owners and trainers of the original Lassie (who appeared in seven MGM films between 1943 and 1951). When Weatherwax applied for his Social Security card in 1935, he listed his occupation as "animal trainer."

In the poppy field sequence (in which Dorothy falls asleep) the realistic-looking "snow" used in camera shots was a mix of chrysotile or "white asbestos" and mica silicate. Inflammable and cheap, the mix was widely used as fake snow and sold commercially for holiday displays. During World War II, the need for asbestos for shipbuilding put an end to the decorative use of asbestos, but not before exposing millions of people to harmful airborne fibers in their homes and businesses. Another film of that era, *Holiday Inn*, showed singer Bing Crosby with white asbestos "snow" falling as he sang "White Christmas." (In 1946, working with Russell Sherman, RKO studio's head of special effects, director Frank Capra developed a sprayable version of artificial snow by mixing foamite, a material used in fire extinguishers with sugar, water, and soap flakes to make Bedford Falls look like a winter wonderland in *It's a Wonderful Life*).

For the poppy field sequence, stagehands used 40,000 artificial flowers to cover the floor of the set on Stage 29. (Poppies often appear on tombstones to symbolize eternal sleep. In the story, the magical poppy field on the way to Oz threatens to make the protagonists sleep forever). When the characters awake and are skipping out of the poppy field, Judy nearly trips and holds on to the Scarecrow to avoid falling.

Albert Arnold "Buddy" Gillespie, the genius behind the special effects of *Oz*, joined MGM as a set designer in 1925, a year after it was founded. He was educated at Columbia University and the Arts Students League. His first project was the original silent film version of *Ben-Hur*, released that same year. In 1936, he became the head of the studio's Special Effects Department, working on more than 400 major feature films and earning twelve Academy Award nominations and four Oscars. (Gillespie directed MGM's logo title sequences featuring Leo the Lion, shot by cinematographer Harold J. Marzorati).

The tornado scene in *Oz* ranks as one of the most realistic storm sequences in movie history, yet its creation was rather simple. When Buddy Gillespie remembered that wind socks at airports resembled the shape of a tornado, he decided to make a 35-foot-long canvas stocking affixed to a gantry crane, keeping it flexible so that it could bend, twist, and move from side to side. By rotating the top and bottom in opposite directions, the "tornado" appeared to snake back and forth, while wind machines created the illusion of both wind and dust. The result was the remarkable tornado sequence, at a cost of $12,000 the most expensive special effect in the movie. (MGM re-used various takes of the sequence in *Cabin in the Sky* in 1943 and *High Barbaree* in 1947).

To produce the illusion of a real tornado, Gillespie sprayed powdery carbon and sulfur particles from both the top and bottom of the muslin sock with compressed air hoses. And since the muslin was porous, some of the dust mixture came through the material providing an even more realistic appearance. Once the "tornado" had been filmed, the effects department used rear-screen projection behind the actors. As Dorothy and others moved around the stage, wind machines blew dried leaves and other debris thrown onto the set by stage hands.

For the tornado sequence, Dorothy's house was a miniature, barely a foot wide. To simulate the house falling from the sky, the model was dropped to a stage floor painted to look like the sky, and the resulting footage was run backward. The "Surrender Dorothy" skywriting scene used a tank of water and a tiny model witch attached to the end of a long hypodermic needle. The syringe was filled with milk, the tip of the needle was put into the tank and the words were written in reverse while being filmed from below.

"A horse of a different color" metaphorically represents something that may be completely separate from what one originally expected. According to American lore, President John Adams used the expression to discuss divided loyalties. For the filming of *Oz*, four Welsh Mountain Ponies were used to create the effect of an animal that changes color from moment to moment (the filmmakers found that multiple color changes on a single horse were too time-consuming). The Humane Association refused to allow the horses to be dyed, and, instead, technicians tinted the animals with liquid gelatin to create a spectrum of colors, white, yellow, red, and purple. Shooting had to be done quickly because the horses would constantly try to lick their fur.

It took the art department over a week to decide the shade of yellow for the Yellow Brick Road, finally settling on several layers of basic yellow house paint purchased from a hardware store several blocks away from the studio. (The gray circle and zig-zag pattern interrupting the yellow brick road outside the main entrance of Emerald City spell out "OZ").

She had hoped to work as an actress in Hollywood, but became a negative cutter and then a film editor at MGM. When sixty thousand feet of *Oz* footage was to be trimmed to a finished six thousand, it would be up to Blanche Sewell to see that the soul of a story did not end up on the scrap floor. (Blanche was the sister-in-law of Walt Disney).

Thanks to his sister, Norma (one of MGM's biggest stars of the era) Douglas Shearer was hired as a stagehand, and when the studio began making sound pictures, he was appointed head of the sound department. As sound editor for *Oz*, his challenge was putting in up to twelve tracks of sound in some scenes at a time when most movies had three. His team went to Catalina Island and recorded thousands of birdcalls, then played them at different speeds and backwards to achieve the unearthly shrieks of the Witch's haunted forest. Other special sound effects included the rustle of the Scarecrow's straw, the Tin Man's metallic clanks, the Lion's roars, and Toto's growls and barks. He worked closely with vocal arranger Ken Darby to create the distinctive sound of the Munchkins.

The attack of the flying monkeys required the hanging of 2,200 piano wires from the sound stage's ceiling. Harnesses were used to move actors around in the flight scenes, such as the flying sequences of the Winged Monkeys, and the broom ride of the Wicked Witch of the West. During the haunted forest scene, several actors playing the monkeys were injured when the wires suspending them snapped, dropping them several feet to the floor of the sound stage. (The wings were patterned after the Andean Condor, the largest flying land bird). It was stunt-double Bobbie Koshay, not Judy, who was carried into the air by the monkeys in that scene.

When the Wicked Witch of the West disappears from Munchkinland, fire and smoke erupt, concealing her exit through a trap door and stage elevator. On the first take (the one we see in the film), smoke was released too early. On the second take, the elevator timing was off and flames erupted too soon, setting fire to Margaret Hamilton's huge hat and witch's broom. The grease in her toxic, copper-based makeup melted, and concerned that copper might get into her bloodstream, her makeup was quickly and painfully removed with alcohol and cotton balls. After spending six weeks recovering from severe burns to her face and right hand, she returned to the picture. (Cosmetics legend Max Factor had personally formulated and applied Hamilton's green makeup).

When Margaret Hamilton returned to the set after recovering from her burns, she was scheduled for the "Surrender Dorothy" skywriting sequence in which her broomstick billows smoke. She adamantly refused to play in any scene involving fire. Her stand-in, Betty Danko, performed instead, and while seated on a smoking pipe configured to look like a broomstick, the pipe exploded. She spent eleven days in the hospital with a brave extra, Eileen Goodman, finishing the shoot for her. Danko made $790 for her work on the film, plus the $35 she earned for riding the broomstick. The accident left her legs permanently disfigured and scarred.

Originally, Buddy Ebsen (who later played Jed Clampett on CBS's *The Beverly Hillbillies*, a situation comedy broadcast from 1962 to 1971) was cast as the Scarecrow and Ray Bolger was offered the Tin Man role. But Bolger preferred to play the Scarecrow as a tribute to his childhood idol, Fred Stone, who had inspired Bolger's career in vaudeville and had performed the Scarecrow role on stage in 1902. "I'm not a tin performer," explained Bolger. "I'm fluid." He convinced producer Mervyn LeRoy, and Ebsen agreed to trade roles with Bolger. (Although the movie refers to the character as the Tin Man, his name in the *Oz* books is the Tin Woodman).

Agreeing to play the Tin Man was unfortunate for Ebsen, since the "metallic" makeup coated his lungs with aluminum powder. One morning, a week into shooting, he woke up physically unable to breathe. His wife rushed him to the hospital where they placed him in a negative pressure ventilator (iron lung) because his lungs had lost nearly all ability to process oxygen. Ebsen's medical departure caused the film to shut down while a new actor was found to fill the part. Song-and-dance man Jack Haley got the role and as an extra precaution, the makeup crew reformulated the powder into a paste. (Haley later missed four days of filming when the makeup caused an eye infection, but he did not suffer any permanent damage and did not lose his job).

According to the script, after being caught in a rainstorm, the Tin Man's joints had been rusted so badly that he couldn't move for a year, yet Haley's scenes had been filming for three days before anyone realized that he had no "rust" on his "tin" costume. The "rust" was applied, and the cost of re-shooting cost the studio $60,000. (The 40-pound costume was actually silvery leather; its tinny sound effects were dubbed in during post-production). In reality, a Tin Man would never rust – iron rusts, but tin does not – so technically the character is actually an "Iron Man." During his solo dance, the puff of "steam" emitted from his funnel hat was produced by compressed air blowing talcum powder. The "oil" that was used to lubricate the Tin Man was actually chocolate syrup.

Haley chose to use an almost falsetto-like voice when playing the Tin Man, and his normal voice in the character of Hickory, one of the farm hands in Kansas. It was Haley's idea to use the tone of voice he used when reading bedtime stories to his then-small son Jack. (Jack Haley, Jr. was once married to Judy Garland's daughter, Liza Minnelli).

Fred Andrew Stone, who began his career as a performer in circuses and minstrel shows, went on to act in vaudeville, on Broadway, and in feature films. He played the Scarecrow in the 1902 musical stage version of *The Wizard of Oz* and was briefly considered for the role in the movie. However, he had been injured in an airplane crash attempting a stunt and was not physically up to the demands of the role. (In 1939, he appeared on a radio program along with Ray Bolger to promote the film).

MGM makeup artist Jack Dawn developed a synthetic plastic he called "vinylite resin" for which he received a patent. Its first application was used to create the Chinese faces for the mostly white cast of *The Good Earth* in 1937. Dawn was assigned the task of giving life to the Scarecrow, Tin Man, and Lion, as well as the Munchkins, the Wicked Witch of the West, and multiple looks for Frank Morgan's five different characters. (Dawn's cinematic work aided disfigured soldiers of World War II. He worked closely with San Diego Naval Hospital in 1943, creating inlays for hands and faces so that patients could appear normal between multiple plastic surgery operations).

An art major from the University of California, Charles Schram was exclusively assigned to work on Bert Lahr's Cowardly Lion make-up, which included a bald cap, rubber appliances, orange-toned make-up, false eyebrows, black whiskers, a wig with rubber ears and a beard. Lahr's face moulds were so restrictive that he had to eat his meals through a straw.

"They had the qualities they desired all along," the Wizard explains to the Scarecrow, Tin Man, and Lion, but they did not recognize them. To reinforce that idea, he gives them tokens to confirm and symbolize those attributes. After he receives a diploma called "The Honorary Degree of Th.D. (Doctor of Thinkology), the Scarecrow recites the Pythagorean Theorem — incorrectly. He states: "The sum of the square roots of any two sides of an isosceles triangle is equal to the square root of the remaining side." He should have said, "The sum of the squares of the short sides of a right triangle is equal to the square of the longest side."

The scrip originally called for the Wizard to sing as he hands out the awards. The song idea was scrapped on the suggestion of lyricist "Yip" Harburg who felt the scene would work better as a non-musical one, so he adapted the lyrics into prose form.

As one of the Emerald City manicurists, actress Lois January sings to Dorothy that "we can make a dimpled smile out of a frown" and later appears as the rosy-cheeked girl holding the Siamese cat that causes Toto to jump out of the hot air balloon just before it departs, leaving Dorothy apparently stranded in Oz. (In 1942, January became the poster girl for Chesterfield cigarettes). Other Emerald City attendants included Ethelreda Leopold, who later appeared in several motion pictures in the 1930s and 40s, usually playing a showgirl, a cigarette girl or a stereotypical secretary, and Dona Massin, who also worked as a choreographer on the film, assisting dance director Bobby Connolly. She originated the "skip" that was performed down the Yellow Brick Road. Among her other film credits were *I Dood It*, *Flirtation Walk*, *The Charge of the Light Brigade* and *Girl Crazy*.

The film started shooting on October 13, 1938, and was completed on March 16, 1939. It was not the big hit that MGM was hoping for, barely covering production costs on its first release – the price of a child's ticket (usually half) reduced box office receipts, and 1939 was an incredibly competitive year at the movies. The final price tag for *Oz* was $2,777,000 and it grossed $3,017,000 in its first release; it grossed an additional $1,564,000 on its first re-release in 1949 and another $465,000 in 1955 before it began airing on TV in 1956.

L. Frank Baum's widow, Maude Gage Baum, was paid a nominal consulting fee by MGM to help promote the film. She was interviewed on the radio program *Ripley's Believe It or Not* and photographed lunching with Judy Garland and attending the Hollywood premiere.

During filming, Judy studied at the MGM studio school to earn the credits she needed for a high school diploma. When young contract players had passed all requirements, they would attend a local high school for graduation. Although Judy had planned to graduate with the class at Hollywood High School, only a few days after completing shooting of *Oz*, she was sent out on a five-week Personal Appearance Tour with Mickey Rooney and had to forfeit the graduation ceremony.

On August 12, 1939, the film had a "soft opening" at the Strand Theatre in Oconomowoc, Wisconsin, the hometown of Meinhardt Raabe, who played the Munchkin coroner. More glitzy openings were held three days later at Grauman's Chinese Theatre in Los Angeles and on August 17 at Loew's Capitol Theatre in New York City before national release on August 25th. The New York screenings were followed by live vaudeville-style performances by Judy and Mickey Rooney, extended in Rooney's case for a second week and in Judy's to three. They did five shows a day, and one day halfway through their 45-minute performance, Judy collapsed in the wings from exhaustion, forcing Mickey to improvise until she recovered, four or five minutes later.

During the nineteen weeks she spent making *Oz*, Judy received her MGM contract salary of $500 per week, and income for the actual filming came to $9,649.98. However, MGM paid her a bonus of $10,600 for the *Oz* tour.

The MGM publicity machine set out to create a sense of anticipation for the upcoming release of the film. Publicity was lavish, with the studio spending over a quarter-million dollars, not only to keep *Oz* fans informed of the film's progress, but also provide appealing trivial side notes about the production, most of which revolved around the Munchkins. The studio notified Hollywood journalist Hedda Hopper of a satirical incident involving the Munchkins which she described in her column: "The midgets, on going in for fittings for *The Wizard of Oz*, frightened the life out of the desk girl. She heard voices but saw no one until she got up and leaned over the desk and looking down, found three midgets."

Howard Strickling was in charge of the publicity surrounding *Oz*, and also the voice-over announcer on the trailers for all three theatrical releases of the film (1939, 1949, and 1955). At a time when image meant everything and the stars were worth millions to the studio, Strickling was known as a "fixer," covering up scandals, keeping stars out of jail and their names out of the papers.

Photographer for the film's production stills, Virgil Apger joined MGM in 1931 as assistant to studio photographer Clarence Sinclair Bull (known as "the man who shot Garbo"). Beginning on *China Seas* in 1935, Apger's job was shooting publicity stills of the studio's stars. He is noteworthy in Oscar history as well for being the only photographer to receive an Academy Award for Production Stills (*Mrs. Miniver* in 1942). In 1947, he was put in charge of the MGM portrait gallery.

Following the film's opening, Macy's New York department store carried "Judy Garland Dresses" and hats, supposedly "Designed for and selected by Judy Garland herself" for the "Teen Age girls who are exactly Judy's age — growing girls with grown up ideas."

Shirley Temple, MGM's first choice to play Dorothy, was the top box office draw four years in a row from 1935 to 1938 in a *Motion Picture Herald* poll. She dropped to number thirteen in 1939, while Judy Garland zoomed from nowhere to number five after the release of *Oz*.

MGM considered re-uniting the original cast for a sequel. Noel Langley began making notes based on *The Marvelous Land of Oz* (the second of Baum's *Oz* books and sequel to *The Wonderful Wizard of Oz*), following-up on many of the concepts he had developed for the 1939 film. Unlike Professor Marvel's hot air balloon, the idea never got off the ground.

The Wizard of Oz was nominated for six Academy Awards, including Best Picture (producer Mervyn LeRoy), Best Color Cinematography (Hal Rosson), Best Interior Decoration (Cedric Gibbons), Best Special Effects, Best Song ("Over the Rainbow" by Harold Arlen and lyrics by E.Y. Harburg) and Best Original Score (Herbert Stothart). *Gone With the Wind* swept the major categories, leaving *Oz* with the two awards for music. Judy Garland was given a special "Oscar Juvenile Award" for her role, something she later referred to as the "Munchkin Award."

According to the Library of Congress, *The Wizard of Oz* is the most-watched film ever, due in part to its regular broadcast on network TV beginning in the 1950s. Over the past seventy-five years, one billion people worldwide have seen the film.

While *New Yorker* magazine's Russel Maloney dismissed the film as a "stinkeroo," other critics wrote:

"Nothing comparable has come out of Hollywood in the past few years to approximate the lavish scale of this filmusical extravaganza, in the making of which the ingenuity and inventiveness of technical forces were employed without stint of effort or cost."

— *Variety*

"You can see it again and again and never tire of its marvels."

— *The Los Angeles Herald-Express*

"Just sit and look back in wide-mouthed astonishment and admiration."

— *The Chicago Daily News*

"A delightful piece of wonder-working which had the youngsters' eyes shining and brought a quietly amused gleam to the wiser ones of the oldsters; not since Disney's *Snow White* has anything quite so fantastic succeeded half so well."

— *The New York Times*

"Judy Garland makes a delightful Dorothy as she wanders through Oz until she realizes that all the wonderment in the world can be had in her own back yard ... *The Wizard of Oz* is an amusing and spectacular film."

— *The New York Herald Tribune*

"Judy Garland is perfectly cast as Dorothy. She is as clever a little actress as she is a singer and her special style of vocalizing is ideally adapted to the music of the picture."

— *The New York Daily News*

REFERENCES

Baum, Frank Joslyn; MacFall, Russell P. *To Please a Child: A Biography of L. Frank Baum*, (Reilly & Lee, 1961).

Baum, L. Frank. *The Wonderful Wizard of Oz* (Hill, 1900).

Hearn, Michael Patrick. *The Annotated Wizard of Oz* (Potter, 1973).

Scarfone, Jay; Stillman, William. *The Wizardry of Oz* (Grammercy Books, 1999).

Herman, Gail, *The Wizard of Oz Movie Storybook* (Scholastic, 1998).

Harmetz, Aljean. *The Making of the Wizard of Oz: Movie Magic and Studio Power in the Prime of MGM* (Hyperion, 1998).

Langley, Noel. *The Wizard of Oz* (Faber, 1991).

Loncraine, Rebecca. *The Real Wizard of Oz: The Life and Times of L. Frank Baum* (Gotham, 2010).

Meyerson, Harold; Harburg, Ernie. *Who Put the Rainbow in The Wizard of Oz?* (University of Michigan Press, 1995).

Greene, David L.; Martin, Dick. *The Oz Scrapbook* (Random House, 1977).

Main, Darren John. *Spiritual Journeys Along the Yellow Brick Road* (Findhorn Press, 2000).

Nathanson, Paul. *Over the Rainbow: The Wizard of Oz as a Secular Myth of America* (State University of New York Press, 1991).

Clarke, Gerald. *Get Happy: The Life of Judy Garland* (Random House, 2000)

In Invitation

With a view to future revisions, suggestions for additions, corrections of errors, or changes in biographical data are invited.

The publishers cordially invite you to submit your criticisms of this book and any other volumes that bear the History Company name. Ideas for new books or reprints to be added to our catalogue are also most welcome.

Please address your criticisms, corrections, or suggestions to:
support@historycompany.com

Made in the USA
San Bernardino, CA
16 December 2019